Winning Confessions of a DIVA

by Dymeata Burum

WINNING Confessions of a DIVA

Unless otherwise noted, all scripture quotations are from the King James Version of the Bible.

2010

1st Printing
Copyright by Dymeata Burum

bBold Publications
P.O. Box 10913
Merrillville, IN 46411

All Rights Reserved

Printed in the United States of America

Cover Design: Lifted Soul Graphics

ISBN 978-0-578-05187-1

All rights reserved under International Copyright Law. Contents and/or cover may not be reproduced in whole or in part, in any form or by any means without the expressed written content of the Publisher.

Dear God,

Thank you for giving me this wonderful opportunity to share my gifts with the world. There is none like you and I thank you for equipping me daily with the necessary tools to help advance the Kingdom of God. Father, I thank you for birthing this dream through me. I thank you for giving me the confidence and boldness to fully trust in you to pursue my dreams.

Forever Yours,

Dymeata B.

DEDICATION

To my amazing husband Brandon, thank you for your genuine love & support. To my two beautiful daughters Raina-Alexandria and Jada-Victoria. To my wonderful parents *and* Pastors; Charles & Sandra Jones. To my entire Gary Christian Center Church family. I love you all and thank you for being a part of my life.

Dymeata B.

Table of Contents

Introduction	7-8
Daily Diva Confession	9-10
Discover Your Identity	10-11
4 Steps to a Better Self Image	11
Walking In Love	12
Woman of Wisdom	13
Building A Successful Marriage	14
Bearing Children	15
Confession For Your Children	16
The Virtuous Woman	17-18
Saved, Single & Successful	18-19
Attaining Your Dream Desires	20-21
The Woman of Surplus	22
Living Debt-Free	23
Family Protection	24
The Diligent Woman	25

4 Steps to Staying Diligent	26
Overcoming Compromise	27
Healing In The Body	28
Overcoming Worry & Fear	29
4 Steps to Overcome Worry	30
Living a Balanced Life	31-32
Weight Loss	33
Promotion on the Job	34
Overcoming Mental Depression	35
Overcoming Addictions	36
Overcoming Your Past	37
30- Day WINNING CONFESSIONS	38-39
DIVA'S Keep Winning	40
Daily Diva CONFESSIONS	41-101
About the Author	102

INTRODUCTION

As I began reading God's Word on a consistent basis, my dreams, desires, and my confidence level has increased. As my father would always say, "Your tongue is the prophet of your life". I would hear that over and over, until one day it made sense to me. I had come to the conclusion that my life would only go as far as my confessions would take me. So today, I'm asking you, what are you speaking over your life? What destination does your tongue have you arriving to? God desires to show His manifested glory through our lives, but He cannot do it until we adjust what we confess over our lives. Ladies, don't make your Christian walk so complicated. Our job is easy, we are to:

ASK -BELIEVE –CONFESS -DECLARE -EXPECT

That's it!!! We must **ask** Him according to His word, **believe** when we ask. **Confess** His Word with our mouth on a daily basis. **Declare** it to those we fellowship with, and **expect** it to be manifested in our lives. God desires for us to increase in every area of our lives. As you increase your word level, you will increase your faith level. I pray that we end up at the same destination…*The Winning Zone*!

Keep WINNING,
Dymeata B.

Daily Diva Confession

I AM...DRIVEN
I AM...INFLUENTIAL
I AM...VICTORIOUS
I AM...ASSERTIVE

I AM A D.I.V.A.

I am blessed because I fear YOU and walk in YOUR ways. Lord I trust in YOU, and because I trust in YOU, I am like Mount Zion which cannot be removed, but I will stand forever. God, YOU are my help; and my help is in YOU. You give me grace to handle *every* situation that I face today.

I thank you that I am in hot pursuit for you and always chasing after you. I consistently meditate in YOUR Word. I thank you that your Word is a lamp unto my feet, and a light unto my path. I declare that my steps are established and I succeed; and everything I put my hands to do will prosper.

I believe that I *am* blessed, and it's just a matter of time before things change in my life, and what I see now is only temporary.

Today I choose to be the D.I.V.A. that you have called me to be! In Jesus Name, Amen!

Discovering your Identity

I KNOW who I am…

…because I believe that my appearance should be a reflection of Jesus Christ. I walk with confidence and assurance of Christ being with me *and* in me. My self- perception and attitude towards life lines up with your Word. I am changing the way I think and speak, therefore I am transforming the way I live. Lord, your Word declares that I am fearfully and wonderfully made in your image. My physical appearance is a reflection of your glory. I am virtuous, holy, presentable *and* acceptable in your eyes. I identify with the beautiful image of your Word. I am elevating in every area of my life. I live an excellent life because I KNOW WHO I AM!

In Jesus name, Amen!

4 STEPS TO A BETTER SELF IMAGE

Take out the garbage- Begin renewing your mind of the distorted perception of yourself. Only speak and believe what God says about you.

Examine yourself- Take time to look at yourself in the mirror or write down the wonderful things about you that makes you unique. List your gifts, talents and positive things that you like about yourself.

Run *your* race- Stop comparing yourself with other people. There will always be someone who *have* more than you. You will never appreciate who God made you by comparing yourself to other people.

Just Say Thank You- Have you ever received a compliment and replied," Girl, this old thing, I had this for years." When you reject a compliment, the message you give about yourself is that you are not worthy of the acknowledgment. Just say "Thank You".

Walking In Love

TAKING A LOVE WALK

Father in the name of Jesus, I make a decision to walk in love today. I confess right now that I endure long, and I am patient. I will not envy or be jealous, I am not boastful or proud. I am not rude or act unbecomingly. I thank you that my hopes are fadeless under all circumstances, and I endure everything without giving up because my love never fails.

Father, I confess the love of God over those who persecute me, and I bless those that curse me. I am not easily offended, but I am filled with the fruit of the spirit. I confess that everywhere I tread my feet I am sowing seeds of love. And as I walk in love and wisdom, people around me are being blessed by my life. I expect favor with others because I choose to walk in love.

In Jesus Name, Amen!

Becoming a Wise Woman

The words of wise men are heard in quiet more than the cry of him that ruleth among fools.
Ecclesiastes 9:17 (KJV)

I AM A WISE WOMAN WALKING…

And by faith, and I declare that *it* is working, because I acknowledge every good thing which is in me through Christ Jesus. I hear your voice, and the voice of the stranger I will not follow. Lord, your will is being manifested in my life, and I live a life that is pleasing to you. I walk in wisdom, knowing what to do in every situation in my life.

I totally depend on you Lord, and make my thoughts to line up with your will, so that my plans, actions, and desires are established and succeed. I trust that you are ordering my steps and making them sure, I enter into your rest by trusting and relying on you.
In Jesus Name, Amen!

MARRIAGE CONFESSION

Marriage is not a noun; it's a verb. It isn't something you get. It's something you do. It's the way you love your partner every day.
~Barbara De Angelis

Father, we thank you that we live and conduct our marriage and ourselves with an excellent spirit. We commit ourselves to live in peace with one another, and delighting in each other. I declare that we are gentle, compassionate, and tender-hearted. God I know that you are perfecting those things that concern us. Right now, I let go of all bitterness, insecurities, and evil thoughts. I am ready to forgive just as you have forgiven me. Because we follow after love and dwell in peace, our prayers will not be hindered in the Name of Jesus. Our marriage is growing stronger day by day. I decree that our marriage is a model for this generation! Father, I thank you for the manifestation.

In Jesus Name, Amen!

BEARING CHILDREN

> When a child is born, there are two births: the birth of the child and the birth of the mother.
> ~ Laura Ramirez

I thank you Lord that you are granting my husband and I with the ability to bear children. Your Word declares that you give children to the childless wife, so that she will become a joyful mother. You are increasing my family and giving us our hearts desires. As your inheritance through Jesus Christ, I receive your gift, which is the fruit of my womb. So right NOW, I call my womb blessed.

I praise you because I know that I receive of you whatsoever I ask because I keep your commandments and do what is pleasing in your sight. I thank you that we are fruitful in our household; and our child/children will be like olives planted around our table. I confess that my children will serve the Lord all the days of their lives.

In Jesus Name, Amen!

Confession for Your Children

Father I thank you that my children are a reward from You, and I give you praise because you add NO sorrow to Your gifts. I teach Your ways to my children; when I sit in my house, and when I am walking by the way, when I lie down, and when I rise up. I declare, that all things go well with me and with my children, because we choose to do what is right in the sight of You. Your righteousness is with my children's children, because they fear and obey you. And they are saved and will live for you forever. My children will never see lack, and everything they set their hands to do will prosper.

In Jesus Name, Amen!

Daily Diva Scriptures: Psalms 103:17; Deuteronomy 6:7; Deuteronomy 11:21; Deuteronomy 12:25-28; Deuteronomy 30:19

Becoming a Virtuous Woman

THE "Proverbs 31" DIVA

DRIVEN-INFLUENTIAL-VICTORIOUS-ASSERTIVE

I am a driven, influential, victorious, and assertive woman. I am loyal to my *own* husband and I respectfully serve him. I am not zealous, or overanxious. I am spiritually balanced and emotionally strong. I walk in love and compassion and agreement with my husband. I walk in wisdom and build my house on a firm foundation.

I make quality decisions based on the Word of God and not based on my emotions. I am a virtuous woman who is a crown to my husband. I am supportive of my husband and I protect my personality while responding to his desires.

My husband gives me what is due of me and I am fair to him and I share my increase with my husband. I will never put my husband to shame. I am clothed with strength and dignity and my position in my household holds great value. I choose to conduct my household with wisdom. I am known in the gates as a woman with an excellent spirit. Lord, I thank you that you are perfecting those things that concern me.

In Jesus Name, Amen!

Living Saved, Single, and Successful

Before I met my husband, I would always wake up in the middle of the night and pray and just talk to God. And as I prayed, I began to write down everything that I desired in a man of God. After I wrote down my vision of what I desired in my future mate, I didn't go looking for a husband. I continued to live out my purpose. I was confident that God was already preparing my man of God. God said that He would perfect those things that concerned me. We as women, get so distracted in having a "man", that we forget about fulfilling what God has called us to do. You have a part and God has a part. Just do your part. Ladies, let's begin to live our lives with purpose and fulfillment.

SINGLE BUT NEVER DESPERATE...

Father, I thank you that you are Lord over my spirit, soul, and body. I choose from this day forward to live a life of a winner. I am pure in heart, because your Word declares that those who are pure in heart shall see you. I thank you that you are purifying me so that I may see you and hear you more clearly. Today, I choose to walk in the spirit because the lust of the flesh has no power over me. Every day I am being led by the Holy Spirit because you promised that the steps of a good man are ordered of the Lord. So today I decree that I live a fulfilling, and successful single life through Jesus Christ. Lord I thank you that the perfect mate is being prepared for me right now. I am not anxious and I will not move before my time. From this day forward I will keep myself pure and Holy until marriage.

In Jesus Name, Amen!

Attaining Your Dream Desires

Dreams DO Come True

Every great dream begins with a dreamer. Always remember, you have within you the strength, the patience, and the passion to reach for the stars to change the world.
-Harriet Tubman

Lord your Word says, in Matthew 11:22-24 that if I ask anything according to your will you hear me and grant the petitions I ask of you. Therefore, I ask you for the following dream desires and believe that I receive them SUPER-SIZED in my life today. Right now I ask you for the resources that I need to start my **(Business/Product Name)**. I thank you that every day you are giving me another answer to getting **(Business/Product Name)** to the next level internationally. I thank you for the opportunity to speak with Presidents; Vice Presidents; and CEO's of large companies to market my **(Business/Product Name)** I thank you that companies, celebrities, and consumers all over the world are desperate patronize my **(Business/Product)** from the north, south, east, west, and the far places of the earth. I thank you that my dreams are being financed and making money for me. Right now I ask you to give me uncommon wisdom and favor with men and women all over the world who have my answer to take help take me to the next level. I will **NEVER** doubt the dream that you have put inside of me. No dream thief, dream killer, or momentum stealer can sabotage the desires of my heart.

I am being supernaturally blessed, so that I may be a supernatural blessing to the Kingdom and to others. My family will always soar to a higher level in you. I declare that I will never see lack another day in my life, and EVERYTHING I put my heart, my mind and my hands to do will ALWAYS PROSPER!! In Jesus Name, Amen!

The Woman of Surplus

I WILL PROSPER…

Father, you said that if I seek first the kingdom of God and your righteousness, all things will be added to me. So today, I decree that I will never see lack another day in my life. You promised to supply all of my needs according to your riches in glory by Christ Jesus. I *will not* live below my covenant rights *any* longer. I speak light into my situations today. **Lack of clothing I speak to you. Lack of finances I speak to you. Lack of food I speak to you. Lack of transportation I speak to you.** Increase finds its way to me. Favor finds its way to me. I command all natural and spiritual blessings to come upon me and overtake me. And because you make all grace abound towards me, I have all sufficiency in every area of my life to give to every good work. I am a giver and a sower in the Kingdom of God, and from this day forward, I will ALWAYS prosper!
In Jesus Name, Amen!

Daily Diva Scriptures: Jeremiah 1:12; Psalm 91:1-2, 10-11, Psalm 34:7; Proverbs 22:6

Winning OVER Debt

I LIVE A Debt-Free life...

because your Word says that you delight in the prosperity of your servants. I declare that I am debt-free right now. Your Word declares that I am to owe no man anything but to love him. As I continue to build my faith in becoming financially free, I expect to receive unexpected income and debt cancellation. I thank you that I prosper in every area of my life, and all of my needs are met and I come behind in no good thing. I thank you that my bank accounts overflow with abundance, and I am free to give to those in need.

I come against all oppression in my life and declare that I have supernatural protection against the devourer. I command my angels to go now and bring to pass my financial soundness and wholeness. Father, I thank you that I am a wise and faithful steward over my finances. I walk in manifested abundance and I live a debt-free life! In Jesus Name, Amen!

Daily Diva Scriptures: Romans 13:8; Romans 10:17; Psalm 112:3; Philippians 4:19

Family Protection

MY FAMILY IS PROTECTED…

because your hand of protection is over me & my family. I know that You watch over Your Word to perform it, therefore, I cover my family with the Blood of Jesus. Father, you are our refuge and our fortress and no evil shall befall us; no accident will overtake us nor will any plague or calamity come near our dwelling. Today, I release my angels to go forth and surround me and my family. Protect us in all our ways. Father, You are my confidence, whom shall I fear? You keep our feet from being caught in a trap or hidden danger. Jesus, You are my safety!

In Jesus Name, AMEN

Daily Diva Scriptures: Jeremiah 1:12; Psalm 91:1-2, 10-11; Psalm 34:7; Proverbs 22:6; Psalm 112:7; Proverbs 3:26,; Proverbs 3:23-24; Isaiah 26:3; Psalms 3:5, 4:8, 127:2, 149:5; Isaiah 49:25

The Diligent Woman

Being diligent sounds elementary to some, but it didn't come easy for me. From keeping a consistent work-out regiment, to staying on task with a major project, it takes diligence. Before I made reading a consistent habit in my life, I would begin reading a book for a week and would never finish it, no matter how interesting the book may have been. I could never complete my daily tasks. Finally, I got tired of living a life of incompletion. So I decided to confess this over my life.

I CAN FINISH MY RACE...

...because your Word declares that the diligent hands make me rich. I have decided that *whatever* I do, I will do it whole heartily as unto you, knowing that my reward comes from you. I am not lazy or slothful. I will not yield to the temptation to sleep, when I should be working or praying. I thank you that I *am* diligent and I seek to do good. I declare that whatever I put my hands to do will always prosper.

In Jesus Name, Amen!

Daily Diva Scriptures Ecclesiastes 9:10-11

4 Steps to Staying Diligent

Decide Your Plan-You must be willing to make a quality decision on what the goals are and how you will pursue them.

Commit to the Plan- You must evaluate your time and responsibilities so that you are able "stick with it".

Make a Plan of Action- Take time out to schedule how you will be able to spend your time to pursue your goal.

Stay in the Game- More than likely you will get off track from time to time. When you do, get back on track with your plan.

Don't Give Up- The great thing about consistency is that as you pursue it, you will see results. But you will never see them if you give up on them.

Overcoming Compromise

I will NOT Compromise…

Heavenly Father; There are areas in my life that I have not fully surrendered to You, Lord Jesus. Lord, forgive me for compromising the Word of God. Today, I pull down every stronghold without reluctance or willful deception in my heart. By the power of the Holy Spirit, I bind every satanic spirit that were reinforcing compromise and sin within me. I thank You Lord, for forgiving me and cleansing me from all my sins and areas where I have compromised. And by the grace of God I make a commitment to myself to follow through in these areas:

(Name your areas)

In Jesus Name, Amen!

Healing In Your Body

Prospering In Your Body

Beloved, I wish above all things that thou mayest prosper and be in health, even as thy soul prospereth.
3 John 1:2(KJV)

Lord I thank you that I walk in divine healing because it is your will for me to live and not die. Lord you are the same yesterday, today, and forever, and your Word *never* changes. You came that I may have life and have it to the fullness. Therefore, I speak to every germ, sickness, disease, and infection and command it to die in Jesus Name. I declare that I will prosper and be in good health, even as my soul is prospering. I am disciplined and possess self control. No weapon formed against me shall prosper. _____, you cannot rest in my body! I thank you Lord that I have exactly what I have prayed for today. I know that you are perfecting that which concerns me in Jesus Name, Amen!

Daily Diva Scriptures: John 10:10; Prov. 4:22; I Peter 2:24; Joel 3:10; Hebrews 13:6; Acts 10:38

Overcoming Fear & Worry
Don't Worry, Be Happy!

Worry is the act of being preoccupied with something you cannot control.
~Pastor Charles Jones

Lord, you have not given me a spirit of fear, but power love and a sound mind. By faith I receive a calm, peaceful and relaxed spirit. I commit every worry, care, and anxious thought, to you. I am confident that you are perfecting those things that concerns me. Nothing but the peace of God is ruling in my heart and mind today. I thank you that when I lie down to rest tonight, my situation is already working in my favor. I choose to rest in you today.
In Jesus Name, Amen!

Daily Diva Scriptures: Psalms 4:8; Isaiah 26:3; Proverbs 3:24; Psalms 127:2;

4 STEPS TO OVERCOME WORRY

In today's society, worry and fear is a major problem. Women, we can't afford to live in worry and fear, because it takes years off of our lives. The bible says that "a relaxed attitude lengthens a man's life." Jesus himself said, "Don't worry about things, such as your food, drink and clothes ... don't be anxious about tomorrow. Ladies, be encouraged, and know that God will take care of *you*. Sometimes we allow the urgency of our circumstances to rob us of our peace. It is one thing to *know* about God's peace, but it is another thing to *experience* His peace.

Relax- Worry depletes your energy and can even cause physical illness.
Release- Forgive yourself and others for mistakes of the past that has triggered you to worry. **Repeat-** Instead of talking doubt and unbelief, speak the Word of God over your circumstances. **Reflect-** Thank God for what He has done in past times. Take time to think on the faithfulness of God.

Living a Balanced Life

Lord I thank you for creating me on purpose and with a purpose. I know that you desire for me to walk in total wholeness. I confess today, that my life is well balanced. I live a life that is well pleasing to you. Today, I choose to live balanced in every area of my life. Guard me from those things or people that may try to prevent me from reaching my goals and achieving the dreams that you have put in my heart. I declare on today that I am productive and goal oriented and always busy doing what pleases you.
In Jesus Name, Amen!

3 Steps to Living a Balanced Life

I believe it is very necessary to live a balanced lifestyle. Maintaining balance and staying healthy are one of the most important things a woman should strive do.

Here are 3 simple steps on how to start living a balanced life.

Get Active- Exercise is the most effective way of living a balanced life. Make it fun!

Get Out and Play- Living a balanced life requires you to take time off from work every once in a while. Go to the movies; Go out to eat with your friends. Playing doesn't have to be expensive. Just take time out to relax your mind.

Get Rid of Bad Habits- Living a balanced life is simple, once you make a decision, rid yourself of smoking, drinking, and overindulging. Don't allow yourself to be defeated by your excuses. Set goals and do what it takes to keep yourself healthy and happy.

Weight Loss

"Never, never, never, never give up." ~Winston Churchill

Father, I thank you for the desire to lose _____lbs. Lord with you, I know that all things are possible. Your Word declares that life and death is in the power of the tongue, so I will continue to speak life to my body. I will no longer use food as a substitute to fill the voids in my life. I make wise food choices. And I declare that my health is being restored. My cells, and my metabolism function properly and I am seeing great results. I am consistent to my exercise plan. I will not get discouraged and I will not give up, but I will continue to love myself on this journey.

In Jesus Name, Amen!

Eat Early!

Eat Small!

Eat Slow!

Eat Fresh!

Job Promotion

Lord I know that all power and authority are in Your hands. You turn the hearts of kings wherever You wish. So I thank you that you are speaking to those in authority concerning my promotion. I thank you for giving me favor concerning the next level in my career. You are opening doors for me that no man can shut. Promotion doesn't come from the east, the west, or the south, but promotion comes from you. I thank you that my excellent conduct is setting me before great men and women in authority. Today I declare that I am qualified for promotion. I am confident that you will give me the grace to handle every task that is handed to me. I possess the wisdom, creativity and charisma that is necessary for my promotion. I thank you for it in advance.

In Jesus Name, Amen!

Overcoming Mental Depression

Father I thank you that depression has no place in my life. You died for my infirmities; therefore I walk in victory in every area of my life. I do not allow my present circumstances to dictate my emotional state. Lord, I know that you are in control of my life, therefore, depression and oppression cannot live here any longer. I declare that victory is mine!

In Jesus Name, Amen!

Daily Diva Scriptures: Psalm 55:22; Psalms 31:22-24; Psalms 143:7-8; Mathew 6:26; Matthew 6:26; 2 Samuel 22:29

Overcoming Addictions

Father I thank you that I am free from addiction I let go of drugs and all other things that have held me captive. Never again will I confess that "I can't", because I know that I *can* do all things through Christ which strengthens me. Lord, Your Word says that You have not given me the spirit of fear, but power, love, and of a sound mind. Lord, You always cause me to triumph in Jesus Christ. Therefore, I declare that I am FREE from all addictions.

In Jesus Name, Amen!

Daily Diva Scriptures: II Tim, 1:17; II Cor. 2:14; Isa. 53:5; Matt. 8:17; I Peter 5:7; II Cor. 3:17; Matt. 28:20; Heb.13:5; Phil. 4:11 II Cor.5:21

Overcoming the Past

There are things that we never want to let go of, people we never want to leave behind. But keep in mind that letting go isn't the end of the world, it's the beginning of a new life.
~ Author Unknown

Let Go of Your Past

Father, I have realized that I cannot have a new beginning if I remain stuck in the past feeling sorry for myself. So today, I let go of the past. I let go of past hurts and past failures. Today, I look toward a new beginning in my life. Today is my opportunity for a fresh start. I will NOT look back any longer.

In Jesus Name, Amen!

Daily Diva Scriptures: Matthew 21:22; 2 Corinthians 3:17; Luke 7:47; Hebrews 11:40; 2 Thessalonians 3:16; Psalm 71:20

30 day WINNING CONFESSIONS
In Jesus...

1. I have life and that life is the light of all men. (John 1:4)
2. I have eternal life (John 3:15-16).
3. I have been justified (Romans 3:24).
4. I have peace with God (Romans 5:1).
5. I am loved of God (Romans 5:8).
6. I have an abundance of grace (Romans 5:17)
7. I reign in life (Romans 5:17).
8. I walk in newness of life (Romans 6:4).
9. I am alive unto God (Romans 6:11).
10. I bring forth fruits unto God (Romans 7:4).
11. I have no condemnation (Romans 8:1).
12. I have been made free from the law of sin and death (Romans 8:2).
13. I live by the law of the Spirit of Life (Romans 8:2).
14. I am a child of God (Romans 8:16).
15. I am an heir of God (Romans 8:17).
16. I am a joint-heir with Christ

(Romans 8:17).
17. I freely receive all things from God (Romans 8:32).
18. I am more than a conqueror (Romans 8:37).
19. Nothing can separate me from the love of God (Romans 8:38-39)
20. I am sanctified (1 Corinthians 1:2).
21. I am enriched with all knowledge (1 Corinthians 1:5)
22. I have wisdom (1 Corinthians 1:30).
23. I have righteousness (1 Corinthians 1:30).
24. I have sanctification (1 Corinthians 1:30).
25. I have redemption (1 Corinthians 1:30).
26. I shall be resurrected (1 Corinthians 15:20-22).
27. I have victory over death (1 Corinthians 15:57).
28. All God's promises are "Yes" and "Amen" (2 Corinthians 1:20).
29. I am established and will succeed (2 Corinthians 1:21).
30. I am anointed (2 Corinthians 1:21)

D.I.V.A.'S.... KEEP WINNING!

I pray that you *continue* to exercise your faith by declaring the Word of God over your life. I want to encourage you to declare YOUR faith confessions in your Diva Journal. Ladies, the bible tells us that

NOW faith is the *substance* of things hoped for and the evidence of things not seen. *Your* faith confessions are proof of the "things" you desire from God.

So don't give up, don't quit, don't get discouraged; and *never* go by what you see, because what you see is only temporary. The enemy will try to test your faith by robbing you of your confession, but he is intimidated by the Word of God. As you make daily declarations of the Word of God, and meditate in his Word, He will give you what to say. Just continue to say what God says, and **stay in the winning zone!**

DAILY D.I.V.A. CONFESSIONS

I AM...**D**RIVEN
I AM...**I**NFLUENTIAL
I AM...**V**ICTORIOUS
I AM...**A**SSERTIVE

Confession For: _____

_____
_____
_____
_____
_____
_____
_____
_____
_____
_____
_____
_____
_____
_____
_____
_____
_____

Confession For:_____

_____
_____
_____
_____
_____
_____
_____
_____
_____
_____
_____
_____
_____
_____
_____
_____
_____

Confession For:_____

_____
_____
_____
_____
_____
_____
_____
_____
_____
_____
_____
_____
_____
_____
_____
_____
_____
_____

Confession For:_____

_____
_____
_____
_____
_____
_____
_____
_____
_____
_____
_____
_____
_____
_____
_____

Confession For: _____

_____
_____
_____
_____
_____
_____
_____
_____
_____
_____
_____
_____
_____
_____
_____
_____
_____
_____

Confession For:_____

Confession For: _____

_____
_____
_____
_____
_____
_____
_____
_____
_____
_____
_____
_____
_____
_____
_____
_____
_____
_____
_____
_____

Confession For: _____

Confession For:_____
_____
_____
_____
_____
_____
_____
_____
_____
_____
_____
_____
_____
_____
_____
_____
_____
_____
_____
_____
_____

Confession For: _____

_____
_____
_____
_____
_____
_____
_____
_____
_____
_____
_____
_____
_____
_____
_____
_____
_____
_____
_____
_____
_____

Confession For: _____

_____
_____
_____
_____
_____
_____
_____
_____
_____
_____
_____
_____
_____
_____
_____
_____
_____
_____
_____
_____
_____
_____

Confession For: _____

_____
_____
_____
_____
_____
_____
_____
_____
_____
_____
_____
_____
_____
_____
_____
_____
_____
_____
_____
_____
_____

Confession For:_____

Confession For: _____

_____
_____
_____
_____
_____
_____
_____
_____
_____
_____
_____
_____
_____
_____
_____
_____
_____
_____
_____

Confession For: _____

_____
_____
_____
_____
_____
_____
_____
_____
_____
_____
_____
_____
_____
_____
_____
_____
_____
_____
_____
_____

Confession For:

Confession For: _____

_____
_____
_____
_____
_____
_____
_____
_____
_____
_____
_____
_____
_____
_____
_____
_____
_____
_____
_____
_____
_____
_____
_____
_____

Confession For: _____

_____
_____
_____
_____
_____
_____
_____
_____
_____
_____
_____
_____
_____
_____
_____
_____
_____
_____
_____

Confession For: _____

_____
_____
_____
_____
_____
_____
_____
_____
_____
_____
_____
_____
_____
_____
_____
_____
_____
_____
_____
_____

Confession For: _____

_____
_____
_____
_____
_____
_____
_____
_____
_____
_____
_____
_____
_____
_____
_____
_____
_____
_____
_____
_____

Confession For:_____

_____
_____
_____
_____
_____
_____
_____
_____
_____
_____
_____
_____
_____
_____
_____
_____
_____
_____
_____
_____

Confession For: _____

_____
_____
_____
_____
_____
_____
_____
_____
_____
_____
_____
_____
_____
_____
_____
_____
_____
_____
_____
_____

Confession For: _____

_____
_____
_____
_____
_____
_____
_____
_____
_____
_____
_____
_____
_____
_____
_____
_____
_____
_____
_____
_____

Confession For: _____

_____
_____
_____
_____
_____
_____
_____
_____
_____
_____
_____
_____
_____
_____
_____
_____
_____
_____
_____
_____
_____

Confession For: _____

_____
_____
_____
_____
_____
_____
_____
_____
_____
_____
_____
_____
_____
_____
_____
_____
_____
_____
_____
_____
_____
_____

Confession For: _____

_____
_____
_____
_____
_____
_____
_____
_____
_____
_____
_____
_____
_____
_____
_____
_____
_____
_____
_____

Confession For:_____

_____
_____
_____
_____
_____
_____
_____
_____
_____
_____
_____
_____
_____
_____
_____
_____
_____
_____

Confession For: _____

_____
_____
_____
_____
_____
_____
_____
_____
_____
_____
_____
_____
_____
_____
_____
_____
_____
_____
_____
_____
_____

Confession For: _____

_____
_____
_____
_____
_____
_____
_____
_____
_____
_____
_____
_____
_____
_____
_____
_____
_____
_____
_____
_____

Confession For: _____

_____
_____
_____
_____
_____
_____
_____
_____
_____
_____
_____
_____
_____
_____
_____
_____
_____
_____
_____

Confession For: _____

_____
_____
_____
_____
_____
_____
_____
_____
_____
_____
_____
_____
_____
_____
_____
_____
_____
_____
_____
_____

Confession For: _____

_____
_____
_____
_____
_____
_____
_____
_____
_____
_____
_____
_____
_____
_____
_____
_____
_____

Confession For:_____

_____
_____
_____
_____
_____
_____
_____
_____
_____
_____
_____
_____
_____
_____
_____
_____
_____
_____

Confession For:_____

_____
_____
_____
_____
_____
_____
_____
_____
_____
_____
_____
_____
_____
_____
_____
_____
_____
_____

Confession For:_____

_____
_____
_____
_____
_____
_____
_____
_____
_____
_____
_____
_____
_____
_____
_____
_____
_____

Confession For:_____

_____
_____
_____
_____
_____
_____
_____
_____
_____
_____
_____
_____
_____
_____
_____
_____

Confession For: _____

_____
_____
_____
_____
_____
_____
_____
_____
_____
_____
_____
_____
_____
_____
_____
_____
_____
_____
_____

Confession For:_____

_____
_____
_____
_____
_____
_____
_____
_____
_____
_____
_____
_____
_____
_____
_____
_____
_____
_____

Confession For:_____

Confession For:_____

_____
_____
_____
_____
_____
_____
_____
_____
_____
_____
_____
_____
_____
_____
_____
_____
_____

Confession For:_____

_____
_____
_____
_____
_____
_____
_____
_____
_____
_____
_____
_____
_____
_____
_____
_____
_____
_____

Confession For: _____

_____
_____
_____
_____
_____
_____
_____
_____
_____
_____
_____
_____
_____
_____
_____
_____
_____

Confession For: _____

_____
_____
_____
_____
_____
_____
_____
_____
_____
_____
_____
_____
_____
_____
_____
_____

Confession For:_____

_____
_____
_____
_____
_____
_____
_____
_____
_____
_____
_____
_____
_____
_____
_____
_____
_____
_____
_____
_____

Confession For:　_____

_____
_____
_____
_____
_____
_____
_____
_____
_____
_____
_____
_____
_____
_____
_____
_____
_____
_____

Confession For:_____
_____
_____
_____
_____
_____
_____
_____
_____
_____
_____
_____
_____
_____
_____
_____
_____
_____
_____

Confession For:_____

Confession For:_____
_____
_____
_____
_____
_____
_____
_____
_____
_____
_____
_____
_____
_____
_____
_____
_____
_____
_____

Confession For: _____

_____
_____
_____
_____
_____
_____
_____
_____
_____
_____
_____
_____
_____
_____
_____
_____

Confession For: _____

_____
_____
_____
_____
_____
_____
_____
_____
_____
_____
_____
_____
_____
_____
_____
_____
_____
_____
_____
_____

Confession For:_____

Confession For:_____

_____
_____
_____
_____
_____
_____
_____
_____
_____
_____
_____
_____
_____
_____
_____
_____
_____

Confession For: _____

_____
_____
_____
_____
_____
_____
_____
_____
_____
_____
_____
_____
_____
_____
_____
_____
_____

Confession For: _____

_____
_____
_____
_____
_____
_____
_____
_____
_____
_____
_____
_____
_____
_____
_____
_____

Confession For:　_____
_____
_____
_____
_____
_____
_____
_____
_____
_____
_____
_____
_____
_____
_____
_____
_____
_____

Confession For: _____

_____
_____
_____
_____
_____
_____
_____
_____
_____
_____
_____
_____
_____
_____
_____
_____
_____

Confession For: _____

_____
_____
_____
_____
_____
_____
_____
_____
_____
_____
_____
_____
_____
_____
_____
_____
_____

Confession For: _____

_____
_____
_____
_____
_____
_____
_____
_____
_____
_____
_____
_____
_____
_____
_____
_____

Confession For: _____

_____
_____
_____
_____
_____
_____
_____
_____
_____
_____
_____
_____
_____
_____
_____
_____
_____

Confession For:_____

_____
_____
_____
_____
_____
_____
_____
_____
_____
_____
_____
_____
_____
_____
_____
_____
_____
_____
_____

Confession For: _____

Confession For: _____

Confession For:　_____

About the Author

Dymeata Burum Dymeata is a Gary, Indiana native, she has served in ministry for nearly 20 years alongside her parents, Pastors Charles and Sandra Jones of Gary Christian Center in Gary, IN. After high school, she continued her education at Indiana University Northwest studying Business Administration. Discovering her entrepreneurial gifts, Dymeata is now the founder and Owner of bBold Publications, LadyzRock Boutique, and bBold Cosmetics. Dymeata is the published author of Winning Confessions of a DIVA. She understands that Entrepreneurs are those who don't just talk about what they want to do, but THEY ACTUALLY GET UP and DO IT! Dymeata plans to create a way for other young women to be able to embrace the idea that "anything" is possible, and also showing them how to profit from the things that you love to do. She has a spirit of determination that keeps her going strong, while she continues to walk in boldness. Throughout all of her services, goals, and dreams, one mission remains constant: she continuously seeks to educate, empower, and inspire women throughout her community and beyond by inspiring them to fight to keep their dreams alive. She is truly an example of a woman who lives a dream fulfilled life. She is a devoted wife to Brandon Burum and mother to Raina & Jada Burum.

How has this book inspired you?
Write me at:
Dymeata Burum
P.O. Box 11562
Merrillville, IN 46411

Or log on to: www.DymeataB.com
For speaking engagements or to order more books, you may call (877)242-1574.

www.ingramcontent.com/pod-product-compliance
Lightning Source LLC
Chambersburg PA
CBHW061453040426
42450CB00007B/1337